Though he
to watch a
fall asleep,

The forty days of Lent offer us the
opportunity to respond differently
and wait with Jesus.

Making space to watch and pray
on our own and together can help
us rest in God's love. And it can also
help us think about how much the
world needs us to share that love.

Our prayer is that this Lent may
bring you not only waiting but new
hope.

May we all be encouraged and
supported as we journey together.
And may we meet Jesus, the Lord of
lords, whose day is near.

**Archbishop Justin Welby &
Archbishop Stephen Cottrell**

How to use this booklet

There are 40 actions, one for each of the forty days of Lent, plus one for Easter Day.

For each **week**, there is:

- A **theme**, to help us think about how we can draw closer to God and each other as we wait for Easter.
- A short **Bible passage**.
- A **simple prayer** for use throughout the week.

For each **day** (from Monday to Saturday), there is an **activity**. On some days there are suggested practical actions you and your family or your class at school could take to help others. On others there are challenges to read or listen to Bible stories, reflect, pray and learn more about the theme of *Watch and Pray*.

How many can you do?

There is also an accompanying booklet for grown-ups which also includes daily reflections, as well as a free app with audio.

You can find links to all the print and digital resources for *Watch and Pray* at:
cofe.io/WatchAndPray

Contents

Start of Lent

Waiting with Jesus

During Lent we prepare for the sadness of Good Friday and the amazing joy of Easter Day. On the night before Good Friday, Jesus asked his friends to watch and pray with him. They all fell asleep.

Lent offers us a chance to do better together.

Read

"Then Jesus went with them to a place called Gethsemane; and he said to his disciples, 'Sit here while I go over there and pray … remain here, and stay awake with me.'"

Matthew 26.36–40

Prayer for the week

Lord Jesus, draw close to us this Lent and help us stay close to you. May we trust you in difficult times and happy times. Amen.

Waiting with Jesus

ASH WEDNESDAY

Decide how you will keep Lent this year

Giving or taking something up can help remind us to spend time with God each day as we prepare for Easter.

THURSDAY

Encourage someone having a bad day

A smile, a friendly word or just being there can really help when life seems difficult.

FRIDAY

Spend some time in darkness

Jesus drew close to his Father even in the darkness of the Garden of Gethsemane. Psalm 139 tells us that the darkness is not darkness to God, but the same as the light. How do you feel about the dark?

WEEKEND

Pray for anyone who feels alone

Jesus felt alone and deserted by his friends at times. But God was always with him and is always with us, too.

Week 1

Waiting together

As Christians we believe in one God who made everything and everyone.

This week we explore how we can become more united - joined together - as part of God's family.

Read

"There is one body and one Spirit ... one God and Father of all, who is above all and through all and in all."

Ephesians 4.1-6

Prayer for the week

Loving God, you have created the world and everyone in it. Help us to watch out for signs of your goodness in our world, in other people and in ourselves. Amen.

Week 1

Waiting together

MONDAY

Watch the news today

Notice any stories of people divided from each other. Notice, too, any stories of people coming together to make things better.

TUESDAY

Read Isaiah's vision of a world at peace

Isaiah 11.6-9 imagines God's world at last as peaceful as heaven. What would peace and harmony look like for you?

WEDNESDAY

Sing "He's Got the Whole World in His Hands"

This famous African-American Spiritual celebrates God's love and care for everything and everyone.

THURSDAY
Pray
for people preparing for baptism

At Easter many children and grown ups will begin the journey of Christian faith. Pray for them as they take their place in God's family.

FRIDAY
Thank God for your body

Human bodies are amazing! Give thanks for all your body allows you to do and enjoy each day.

WEEKEND
Try to get to a Communion service

In Holy Communion, we come together to share God's Word as well as bread and wine, and remember that "we are the Body of Christ".

Week 2

Waiting and moving

We are waiting for God to meet us and help us this Lent. But the Bible is full of people who find God as they move about.

So this week we look at how God meets us on the journey.

Read

"The Lord said to Jacob, ' ...Know that I am with you and will keep you wherever you go, and will bring you back to this land...' "

Genesis 28.10–17

Prayer for the week

Faithful God, travel beside us as we go about our daily journeys this week. Guide all our steps and bring us safely home. Amen.

Waiting and moving

MONDAY

Make a list of Bible journeys

From Noah to Mary and Joseph, God often asks people to travel far from home, trusting that God will bless their journeys.

TUESDAY

Pray on the move today

On your journey to or from school, notice the places around you. Say a prayer for the people who live, work and play there.

WEDNESDAY

Read the story of Ruth and Naomi's journey

In Ruth 1.15-22, a young widow chooses to travel with and care for her mother-in-law, Naomi, rather than stay in her own country.

THURSDAY

Think
of a place where you have felt close to God

It's often easy to feel close to God in a church or a cathedral, or out in nature. What places are special to you?

FRIDAY

Remember those taking difficult journeys

Sometimes people are forced to move because of war or lack of food or money. Pray for all travelling in search of safety.

WEEKEND

Watch a film about one of the Bible's great travellers

Joseph: King of Dreams and *The Prince of Egypt* explore great Bible journeys. Can you think of others?

Week 3

Waiting for the Holy Spirit

Before Jesus went back to heaven, he told his disciples to wait for the gift of God's Holy Spirit. This week we explore the amazing difference the Holy Spirit makes to them - and to us.

Read

"Divided tongues, as of fire ... rested on each of them. All of them were filled with the Holy Spirit and began to speak in other languages ... "

Acts 2.1-6

Prayer for the week

Spirit of God, help us to make space this week to wait for you. Bring us new life, new hope and new energy to follow Jesus and serve our neighbour. Amen.

Week 3
Waiting for the Holy Spirit

MONDAY

Listen to a song or hymn about the Holy Spirit

Hymns like 'The Spirit lives to set us free' and Spirituals like 'Every time I feel the Spirit' help us to think about God as Spirit.

TUESDAY

Research how Christians celebrate Pentecost

Pentecost (or Whitsun) is sometimes described as the birthday of the Church. Find out how Christians mark this important day.

WEDNESDAY

Read about the Holy Spirit being given to the disciples

Acts 2.1-8 describes the Holy Spirit giving the disciples strength and courage to tell the world about Jesus.

Pray for more people to become followers of Jesus

Christians in over 85 countries join together to pray "Thy Kingdom Come" each Pentecost. Find out more at thykingdomcome.global

FRIDAY

Share a snack or treat with a classmate

Acts 2.43-47 shows how the Holy Spirit inspired the first Christians to share what they had with others.

WEEKEND

Try to donate to a local foodbank

Many churches help to run foodbanks to make sure no one goes hungry in their community. Is there a local one your household could support?

Week 4

Waiting quietly

Last week we saw how the Holy Spirit came as a rushing wind, helping the disciples to tell everyone about Jesus. This week we explore how God also comes to us in quiet ways, too.

Read

"Now there was a great wind ... but the Lord was not in the wind ... the Lord was not in the earthquake ... the Lord was not in the fire; and after the fire a sound of sheer silence."

1 Kings 19.11-12

Prayer for the week

Lord, help us to be still and remember that you are God. Help us find your peace this week and find ways to share it with others. Amen.

Waiting quietly

MONDAY

Remove your shoes when you can today!

Moses meets God in a burning bush. He takes off his sandals because the ground is holy. In some countries, Christians take off their shoes in church, too.

TUESDAY

Sit in silence for a while

Like Moses, the prophet Elijah hears God's voice on a mountain. But God meets Elijah not in fire but in silence.

WEDNESDAY

Pray for those who feel forgotten

The Book of Job describes bad things happening to a good person. Pray for anyone finding it hard to feel God cares about them.

THURSDAY

Talk honestly to God about your day

This evening, thank God for the good things of today. And bring to God anything that upset or annoyed you, too.

FRIDAY

Include someone who might feel left out

It is good to spend some time quietly on our own. But it's good to talk and have fun with others, too!

WEEKEND

Read or listen to Psalm 46

"Be still ... and know that I am God" (Psalm 46.10). These are good words to say - or sing - to help us remember God is always there, no matter what.

25

Week 5

Waiting for God's help

The Gospels show us many people waiting and hoping that Jesus will help them.

This week we explore how Jesus offers God's healing, forgiveness and peace to those in need.

Read

"And wherever Jesus went, into villages or cities or farms ... the sick ... begged Jesus that they might touch even the fring of his cloak; and all who touched it were healed."

Mark 6.53–56

Prayer for the week

Jesus, we ask you to be close to all who are ill, sad or in trouble, and to bless all who work to care for them. Amen.

Waiting for God's help

MONDAY

Make an Easter card for someone who cares for others

We all rely on doctors, nurses and other healthcare workers when we are ill. Why not suprise one you know with a "thank you" ahead of Easter?

TUESDAY

Read how Jesus helps a man who can't walk

In Mark 2.1-12, a man who can't walk is carried by his friends to Jesus for help. Notice the kinds of help Jesus gives him.

WEDNESDAY

Pray for anyone you know who is unwell

You might want to light a candle (with a grown up's help) as you hold them in your prayers.

Find out about the work of Christian Aid

Christian Aid, Tearfund and other Christian charities help poor communities around the world, inspired by Jesus' care for those in need.

FRIDAY

Look back on how you have treated others today

None of us is always as kind or helpful to other people as we could be! But we can say sorry and ask for God's help to do better tomorrow.

WEEKEND

Take any chances you get to help

Every day brings each of us chances to do something good or kind for others. Try to take any that come your way this weekend!

Week 6 - Holy Week

Waiting for Easter

During Holy Week we wait with Jesus as he shows us just how much God loves the world. We wait together in the sadness. And we will celebrate together when Easter comes.

Read

"He said, 'Jesus, remember me when you come into your kingdom.' Jesus replied, 'Truly I tell you, today you will be with me in Paradise.' "

Luke 23.39–43

Prayer for the week

Jesus, help us to watch and pray with you this Holy Week. Help us trust in you in moments of sadness and praise you in times of joy. Amen.

Waiting for Easter

MONDAY

Plan something nice to do when Lent is over!

We've been watching and praying and we still have a few days before Easter is here. How will you celebrate?

TUESDAY

Make or bake some Easter treats

Get ready for Easter Day by making nests of chocolate eggs, hot-cross buns, simnel cake - or maybe create something new?

WEDNESDAY

Read how Peter lets Jesus down (Matthew 26.69-75)

Peter promised to be a good friend, but when he is frightened he pretends not to know Jesus. Even so, Jesus is still ready to forgive him.

MAUNDY THURSDAY

Thank God for the people who look after you

Before Jesus dies, he asks his mother Mary and his friend John to care for each other like family (John 19.16–27).

GOOD FRIDAY

Pray for anyone grieving this Good Friday

Today we remember Jesus dying on the cross. Ask God to comfort all who are mourning lost loved ones.

EASTER EVE

Think back over the last 40 days

What have you enjoyed about this Lent challenge? What's been difficult? What will you remember?

Easter Day

Celebrate that Easter is finally here!

The long wait of Lent is over. Easter Day is the happiest day in the Church's year. We join together to praise God for raising Jesus to new life.

Happy Easter!